Grim Crack3r's Bars:
The first 3 albums
By rj Longren

ISBN #978-1-716-00950-1

Table of contents

Teaser
Track list image
Mock Track list Top*
Grim Intro
PenneDeath
Ken Doll living
Born again Villain
Blo me
Drink up
Aft3rcare
Ate
Hidden track

Track list Plain
That me in the mirror
Permanent Teenager
Costumes are a Drag
Sorry Santa
Trigger word bit
"prop' version (TFF)

Track list Strays
Out Gold
Two
Third track
Four
Five (previously unreleased)
six/sex
Spelling error
Poor but rich in heartache
a legend

Teaser

My drunken ass less Charles Bukowski
Falling down fishing out my house keys
pretending I was going be a novelist.
Whether or not I would be famous
in that I was not confident
I wasn't Zelda or Fitzgerald, Not Anais , nor June
laying in another's arms as their muse.
Not Miller Swimming in sex journeying to flop
next to the pacific ocean
sharing Steinbeck's devotion
Not Sylvia Plath willing to open the oven,
Lay my face flat on the glass
Could I do Dorthy Parker proud ensnaring wit in
everything I writ ?
Or would I fail to produce the epic fiction I keep
losing interest in?

It makes me lift my pen worried that I will never
write one word again

Swallow that Grim Cracker down
Don't back out now, it's past your lips
Taste his saltiness, I can see you trying to resist
The words right there at my fingertips

Take an intense hit inhale the fragrant prose
Of the bitter after taste of my youthful haste
Those memories I did not escape in type face
Become the lines I fling out in cyberspace

Marshall Mathers - Top

1 Gay for Grim / 2 Written Off / 3 Toy shopping / 4 White Man
Classic Villain / 5 I Do love cupcakes / 6 Sink or Swim / 7
Murder   Husbands / 8 the   first DM

This is clearly a   mock up, it is no way a suggestion   that Marshall
Mathers, AKA the rapper Eminem is in any way involved with or associated with
Grim Cracker AKA the Author rj Longren or their work. This mock album was created
as a show of affection The above tracks will possibly remain unwritten. Hopefully this
statement will help me avoid legal action. Wish me luck.

Unwritten tracks but not unreleased image*

Grim Cracker - bottom

9 Intro to Grim / 10 PenneDeath / 11 Ken Doll Living / 12
Born Again Villain / 13 Blo me / 14 Drink Up / 15 Aft3rcare /
16 Ate

This is clearly a mock up, it is no way to suggest that Grim Cracker is a rapper. It is a
Stan slash fic as the cool kids would say. Not that I was ever cool. If you read this far
there are no prizes. We both know this level of obsession usually ends with a broken
heart and/or legal action, this was supposed to be a disclaimer to help me avoid legal
action. Wish me luck.

First album

Grim Intro

Grim cracker is not a rapper but a device
Nothing but ink slung and lost paradise
A crotch grab with my lip over my teeth
Laying in bed, Drafting bars instead of sleep
Delivering from Mostly my moist rib cage
And I drip, I drip all over this page

Shaken, stirred, baked and assaulted somehow
I'm still bland
We don't have to go to bed for you to rise with me
on your lips
You can be gooey, fluffy, sticky on me
as we get through this shit.

I haven't got time for this pain
 and it's a shame I can't tell you to your face
how the whole thing feels like a sob story
hail to the glory of being
washed in the words of another,
made to serve some singular regular forced gig.
Promised happiness
under work camp conditions kid.
I ain't rolling with the lord
Is the Bible A litter meant to
deliver me to a mass grave,
Bury me in the native blood soaked soil. Saying
"see how we conquered these peoples and we will
do the same to you and yours"

My body is the temple, my body is the sacrifice.
My body is the battle field, my body is vice.
My body is temptation, my body is freedom and
the price.

ideology will never be anything but invisible
it takes mouths to blossom the hatred.
It takes hands to sow
and fertile resentment to spread.
But's all that's been said

I should parade around in a white tank top
Get bleached out by the sun
and let my belt line drop
Check my dick to make sure
 I didn't leave it at home
My pockets are empty, I've blow my load
Playing with the joystick down at the arcade
Trying to stay lost on my way to the grave.

Grim cracker ain't exactly a rapper
I'm a portion of an imperfect whole
white trash somewhat depressed
The queerest son from the midwest

How long will this hatred run on, run on
If I was a singer this might be a song
I'm playing with the words you can follow along
Desperation doesn't deal with perspiration but
I'm swimming in it.
Is it my generation,
is that why we ain't the greatest?
I can't seam to part with one note
nobody gives a shit about anything I've wrote,
darn this stocking, stitch up that rip,
 someone's going notice this bullshit
I've yet to make a dime off any line
So it doesn't matter
that selling my ass got me farther

All out of sugar stuck
sucking a lime over my crusty cherry,
It is a sour juice running through me.
I want to rake someone over the rails
and dangle them by their feet
play live action frogger over a busy street.

Grim Cracker is not a rapper
Not even holding the rest of me down
He's the punk that can spit some junk
If Misery loves company
than I can't be that fucking sad
Up here all alone.

PenneDeath

Murder murder murder on my mind
It's why I put the pen to the paper the first time
Scrawling in pencil helplessly I found true joy
Those mean girls and boys
Let me feed you some poison
Let me cement you in
Becky, Stephanie, Chris and those privileged kids
Murdered, murdered, murdered with my pen.

Poe said nevermore shall you tarry
with this miserable mediocrity
Maybe Modesty isn't
going to pay the bills honestly
I might be like HH Holmes, I am the Ho tale
but I didn't quite reach my full potential
I was never into guns
and I never worked the street
But I'm willing to play Monster
in between the sheets

Murder murder murder on my mind
It's why I put the pen to the paper the first time
Scrawling in pencil helplessly I found true joy
Those mean girls and boys
Let me feed you some poison
Let me cement you in
Becky, Stephanie, Chris and those privileged kids
Murdered, murdered, murdered with my pen.

drowning can happen in three inches
The park had a creek
But I was too slow to catch those nimble bitches
Years later it was more fun

watching them self destruct
Make poor choices a few times
vomiting their guts up
Don't be squeamish they all survived mostly
Perhaps a bit emotionally stu-nted

Men disappoint me in life
Sure it's so great
you can stick your dick in a million times
but how many strokes can you take this knife?
How much arsenic can you handle?
Drink up shit face, you are starting to ramble.

Murder murder murder on my mind
It's why I put the pen to the paper the first time
Scrawling in pencil helplessly I found true joy
Those mean girls and boys
Let me feed you some poison
Let me cement you in
Becky, Stephanie, Chris and those privileged kids
Murdered, murdered, murdered with my pen.

The ink's not dry, there is more blank paper
Fill it up with red, red , red pen pulpy anger
I don't have to wish you would
because you already did
Shitty demented fucking gross popular kids

Ken Doll Living

Spending hours on a dream body, perfect anatomy
Barely a preteen it has stuck with me
that plastic fantasy
Disjointed self image, American chastity
Shiny happy face painted on the man
Barbie had a dream house but I was a ken fan

Can I be your arm candy?
Does my head need to be empty?
Where ever you go, won't you take me?
I'll Walk around your place naked,
bend me over the couch, I can take it
smile for the flash bulbs, full page spread
Ken Doll Living to be the little spoon in bed

It's all about that ass, the grass and the sass
A face down day and the night of a million grunts
bounce some coin start a fuss
Take a dive in the pool I'll belly up to you
Thirsty Grim cracker wrapping his lips around
All the extra words I use to tease
before I please the crowd

Born again Villain

Ken Doll living as a born again villain
People might be tripping jealousy written
Face freshly bitten, tie up your laces, kitten
If I'm a born again Villain,
My booty shorts will be Vermillion
& My tears will be Crocodilian

Someone decided before I was Born
That the only place I am reflected is Porn
Somehow it's not that satisfying to be a Unicorn
Instead of support there is Scorn

Disconnected disco tech dicks
tracking me through an app
My immortal leftovers as I flirt with death
Find something to love and then let it kill you
But how will that work as a born again villain

Was it that I was a hopeful stray?
So why was I hoping to be taken away
Was I starving for love? Hunting all over
To be washed in the affections of another?
White knight, hero or abductor I prayed
Come take me, pick me up, lead me astray

Born again villain take my word for it
Before I left the womb I was marinated in sin
Popped out with a crooked ass smile
This long game will only end when I lose my life
Until then I'll take a spin,
keep using a fork and knife
On this deep shit I am in.

BLAME

Am I a silly Faggot hoping to be heard?
Is my word play not the part that is absurd?
Wipe that look off your face this belligerent mouth
Is loaded up and ready with some click bait

I'm that Faggot and if it's on your lips
then it's on your mind
you can get on your knees ,
start begging for my dick, Say please
Please faggot let me worship your schtick
Let me shoot my shot and give you this lip

Am I a silly Faggot flirting with crayons?
Are my lucky charms
raising your dressing gown?
Is your whole life about laying dick down?
I ain't putting it in your mouth, I'm pulling it out
Gayness ain't contagious but hatred is
It goes from cheap shot to body count

If rap is talking shit more people would compost
You think I'm starting a fight
but it's a wish meat cosmos
If I keep running into you in my subconscious
Then how is it? you exist in the flesh
I must be taking my own delusions out of context
I'm looking for that sugar high inflated ego
Feeling like a Stan, Foaming at the mouth
I need to get a hold
On the back of your head Daddy
get your knee pads ready

I'm that new flavor you been searching for
2014 is going haunt me until I kick it to the curb
Am I a silly Faggot melting your self control?
Grim Cracker is an asshole
A tight little fucker squeezing out nuggets
too small to make tater tots
he's baked graceless,
too much melodrama for a zipless fuck
Dragging my ass out of the cess pool to gaze
At the nostalgia I dug up, then set ablaze
You can be my bitch
for enough cash I'll be that bitch
If you like it, we will switch,
you can be my private dancer
Curl that sneering lip,
bare a few teeth, talk dirty to me
Admit to that desire to service me top
Use that cabbage to get what you want
What's the price of I love you?
From my lips sport?
Think of the power move, Mallow on this cracker
Two dicks pissing out bars forever after
I'll serve you unlimited ink
on a post it note mirror chain
We'll spend our rage flinging darts
at those sipping champagne
Let the words assault you, batter up the pitch is in
Peanut butter chunky enough to rip the pancake,
I can't take it back, I've said too much,
maybe your ass crack spoiled the last bunch,
Would you do it for a cookie?
I hear you like cup cakes.
Good boy got the gumption
to guzzle a gallon of glue
but he couldn't keep his Fucking mouth shut
I guess the next move is up to you

Drink up

Pour myself into something?
The bottle, the page or my rage?
Tour through my misery, all these gone by days.
The slides labeled vaguely the dates guessed
Lacking cohesion but fresh faced non the less
Do you see me there?
With the pigtails in my hair?
I've already mastered the empty smile
 100 yard stare
Another round in glasses,
a few fingers, rings and glances
None of it lasts, not the liquor or my romances
Put my lips to a few necks,
engaged in a few rounds of risky sex
The siren call a husky sigh of my whiskey breath
Queen lay on my wrist, ace deep in my chest
Pack of strays belted out the tune
all about how I ruined you
Like a sip escaping my lip that gin haze
Fading on film as my head lowered to the table
Do you see me there? Because I still do.
The curves of sweet words in my fable
I am the tower, the moat and clearly unstable
Toast to you, my scars, the gravity marks
Drops on the wood floor of the missed gulps
Slopping out of my mouth,
hot hissing compression
Engulfs the despair and depression
Bore you with nothing, the present,
 the past or love game
Whore taken himself too seriously
Collides with poverty to bring out a new name
Drink up the hostility
Let the pen spit through my teeth

Drink up enough liquor vomit and piss
One more time I will dive into the abyss
That is the misery of my home town
One more time I will crack open my heart
And beg for another round
One more time I will reach out
Pour myself the fifth and finally drown.

Aft3rCare

perhaps I'm gravely mistaken Yours is probably
the wrong tree to be shaken
I can not resist, this possible kiss
Embrace reckless ruin, live out my death wish
If I am but a ghoul not laid in the grave
Then I linger as what ever
tasteless asshat I became
We can play word games, or grown up bad dreams
Maybe ride the love rollercoaster again
We can be boys while loving each other as men
pop the cover off eternity, I raped the dictionary.
Used it loosely with innocence
tore the cover from it's pages,
I left it's undignified remains
Shards of sections, mostly pulp,
 In a naked pile on the book shelf.
Grim Cracker the film flam man,
an under cooked tart
I am what I am without the spinach can,
put through the ringer blocked up my fingers,
 dry me out desert
I'm not the first or the last
to be thrown in the trash
I know my disease, the smell of it,
as I walk it down the street
I walk until it drips out of my pores
and lays on the concrete.
Was that my mouth, saying those words,
was that my mouth upon yours?
I'm no stripper, perhaps a deglazed whore
These are sad attempts to flirt and nothing more.
These little dreams of death
haven't finished me off yet
My love of depravity has woven

a rich painful tapestry
Tap into my stream of consciousness,
Consider it apt that I foolishly flap these lips
When these hands don't hold a pen
The weight of my madness rolls me up again
It is the ink that breathes
and not the hand that wields.
Drown me in that stench of failure
rounding the corner on another year
Might mint you another million
my corpse laying there
Fucking pen stuck up my vein,
flayed out on display
Stop picking through my organs,
 seal my fate why fuck around feeling fake
If I'm an unwrapped forgotten fruitcake.
Don't pout when I leave a bad taste in your mouth.
Doesn't my blood write pretty poetry?
regurgitated perverse refrigerated way back
when machine hits perforated lingering in my
vision stream not so lovely memories
trapped, stacked, racked up vividly leaking
got me nervously blinking.
Is my sobriety fleeting?
 Reverse stream spill this sadness out of me,
sour fills my mouth
let me drink up that
 ludicrous delusion of surviving this,
 marinate me in capitalist,
money might not fucking love me
but it piles up,
that's some nouveau Richie rich shit
scooping out strawberry seeds from my teeth
trying to teach me to talk trash.
 talk about thrills,
my flow is sick

as in it needs paddles and a beat to register,
Grim Cracker is not a rapper,
that is laughable
It's a work of art nothing more sinister.

Ate

literary lit this fairy barely my tenth birthday
Hold on to the ire,
 let it fan my flame higher skipped
Headline ripped from a newspaper
page staged skimmed
Over content mired in toxic sentiment
 let that sit a minute

The pen does not wrestle with me
The ink is not a confessional for you to see
Spilled out inner garble marbled lines
Will not be visible in the performance tonight

let this voice give you closure
There was nothing to see here chew it over
Was it dream, fantasy, madness,
or a flash of brilliant lunacy?
Nobody is breaking the bank to buy poetry

Grim is a dingy developed taste,
furious hands could erase
Curious dinner date leaning agape over the plate
scrap scrap

Is it time to go down that rabbit hole?
Are the forces of good and evil
going fight for my soul?
Whose virtue shall I signal with?
 What clever meme or gif
Does the situation demand?
 Abs grating the word count down
Tweet this post to instagram
these digital feats hashtag falling for the
 I proud capital crowd

Tiktok am I too old to go viral?
It's a platform I know nothing about.
Too long winded, all thumbs, don't at me
I was creeping around the internet on AOL
I miss Tetris and Mario 3,
space invaders on my Tandy
A box of cassette tapes remain faithfully awaiting
the next roving
Fall right in, roots gray tinged,
take it back cast away my longing
On the road again,
 it's not I can't wait
it's that I was hoping for a better fate.

Hidden track

This broadcast is not a test
Grim Cracker is not a rapper
He would a firm guiding hand
from Marshal Mathers
Better breath control,
and to hold more than a microphone.
But to suggest this is ridiculous,
I am nobody, an unknown Stan
Not even God could could explain
what may lay dormant in my brain
Grim Cracker is taking a shot, late or not
On surviving beyond a hot meal and a cot
We're all little shady sometimes with past lovers,
others and even family
If they can't accept me
then I don't give a fuck frankly
My trans ass is non binary
it means if you want in my jeans,
you come correctly
Learn my pronouns honey
don't be engaged in fuckery
If U want to be my Daddy
bring me all the words plenty
Sweet, nasty, maybe hot in my ear,
don't gaslight me
If I stole your heart then be proud of my art,
show me love
Hold my hand,
scare the fuck out of those intolerant ones
You know who is going rise again,
it ain't the south
unless we talking about that pole in your pants.
Hi my name is...the reigning king of controversy?
Hi my name is... did you miss me?

At 42 perhaps I'm the answer to your universe
Grim Cracker, a vanilla milkshake
left out in the heat
Sad, melted unexciting white man
A bland cracker crumbling moist
crushed into crust
Cutting the sweet piling up fluffy bullshit
people been pedaling
Selling a million dollar dream helping them fund
their get rich quick scheme.

This is America where you are free to die poor
Given kernels of hope without promise of more
Diet of gluttony left starving for compassion
Will you not tear down the oligarchy?
Will you not follow through with a full revolt?

No I think not, I see all the shiny morsels
Pretty but not enough
fed to the mad mob to sing them off to bed
Lay down your cries of discontentment,
be disillusioned instead
Feast your eyes on this screen,
be wowed by the bling

This broadcast is not a test
It is the queerest thing, if you can't hear it then
it's the algorithm
shuffling me off into the void
with ghosts notifications.

Plain

Grim Cracker

Track List

That me in the mirror
Permanent Teenager
Costumes are a Drag
Meat Popsicle
Sorry Santa
Trigger word Bit
'Prop' Version (TFF)

Second album

That me in the mirror

It's that me in the mirror
I should lay my hands on
Letting my farmer's tan
charm me out of my pants,
drink from the carton
a few calories I can skate off.
The pavement hasn't softened
nor the pen I caution
I'm not mellow but I'm okay as an alone fellow
I don't have the weight
to fling my dreams any further
Letting the sour carve out my body
Casting pearls of inspiration into something
heftier than nocturnal emissions
These haunted renditions on repeat
keeping my sleep at bay
lay between the masses of my restless hands
Is it that garbage I eat?
I should take better care of that me in the mirror
That queer little freak needs to keep their chin up,
have hope and a few better weeks.
The garbage goes somewhere,
I'm still white trash sipping tea
pinky up can't let the crickets get to me

I screen my calls still waiting on Hi
Not quite the dude, no rug to lose
sandals not the resort I had hoped to reach
When I began recording my words into air
thinking I was a clever bitch
I don't have the hunger maybe or is my anxiety?
Will I survive?
you can turn the channel but this is my reality.

Permanent Teenager

The origins of Grim come from way back when
My brother told me my lines had to rhyme
But I know what I was interested in
The form, the structure,
the rules of literature I bend

Destroy me like any true believer would
The big GOD wants me to OD on his love
Smother me in the testaments
as if trans didn't exist in prehistorical texts

You can see me now,
send down the rain crack my skull in
It's those believers making hatred
something to share with their kin
Claiming free speech
 while they pound away at my autonomy
You're jealous
and still jerking off to trans pornography
Permanently a teenager flipping off the hypocrisy
Tripping the censors as I sneak into mentions
My white little fingers smudging up the record

I gave birth to lingering texts of outrage
Shape my narrative with hope spilling on the page
How could I become an adult
 in a world unwilling to see me as a child?
How could I flourish
with out nourishing all the sour I have compiled?

Grim's not some silly cracker,
He's my taste of swagger
Nonchalance dropping foul words
with queer coded proverbs

Why Dress it up if it gets you down
He's a random night on the town
Some wine wasted on a cheesy cracker
served up on a social media platform.

Costumes are a drag

Crayon and robe sketching up this season's garb
Something classic old west
where the leather was beaten and rhinestone less
Enrobed in satin
perhaps the glam diva no man can resist
Poised to upset the power dynamic
with civil unrest
Whether blowing the lawman
or the rancher is anyone's guess
It's love that drives the strong fade with credits

Perhaps don a cowboy hat and chaps
Sling a six inch dong, pop a few beer caps
Far less pageantry more skin to ring in halloween
The one night cis forgive
breaking the gender binary
I can stroll in a three piece suit and heels
Not a stitch of makeup ready to rail
Some friendly nun or priest willing to beg
my forgiveness
I'd ask god but he's busy
while The devil told me I had time to fuck around
We'll find out if he meant it

I'm not your woman but I might be your man
If only for this visit, you can test out my limits
But be wise and don't be hypnotized
I ain't got the time to make you mine

Meat popsicle

Never a pageant contestant,
received enough flyers
Stacked up the pounds
trying to down play the value
Baby fat middle aged men still wanted a piece
of pre transition pre pub Grim
You can blame my emotionally absent father but
he's only part of the problem

I can't tell you the price per pound
of my breast meat,
Only how it was weighting me down

my thoughts ran away with my pen
I meant to form fiction,
to live in a mind palace of my own
Instead I gave away parts like carts
on the Oregon trail leaving their dead
on the prairie
Did my heart make it? Or was it never loaded in?
I imagine my bloated carcass
dangling deep below the waves
The heaviness that keeps me in my watery grave
The same thing that swept me over the side
If I am not useful to the hive
than I am chum for the sharks to come

In death I may be a hero
but in life I am a cautionary tale
Parents will tell their children
that's why there's a binary
They'll leave out all the things
that they voted against, stayed silent about
And chalked up to politics

What a brave meat popsicle
Look at the veins and muscle
Grim Cracker is not an activist,
not some sweet meat on a stick
He's hurling words into your ears
looking for traction.
If you came for a drag show
I hope you have satisfaction
I dragged you into my coffin.
May my corpse be the trend in fall fashion
decaying lips starved bone separating skin
Art is forever but the flesh is a weak vessel.

Sorry Santa

sorry Stacy, Santa doesn't exist.
Your mommy keeps resisting
but I think your father is fisting
her for Christmas.

The jingles are not bells
Dear Steven they are loud yells
Coming from your father who's doing well
Not to come without permission

O the snow's not the only thing dropping
Through out the neighborhood
the cold's not stopping
Anyone from getting it in
behind the bushes at the gym
I hate the holidays especially
when I'm not the one getting laid

Little miss perfect likes a sweet mess
cleaned up by a guest
Mr buttoned up takes turns getting burned
by what ever young thing is visiting
to crap on his chest

Deleted grinder pretending I'm not that ho
Maybe post a few more nearly naked photos.

Santa's into fur,
he likes that whip calls his dears' her
There's eight and from the story
they carry his weight
But I'm the threat because I'm not straight

Sorry I'm not Santa everyone is naughty

Ho ho ho's make money, Stacks of cash
To Be loved by the public. Hide your debauchery
Shine up that nice guy/gal act
 for the media circus
I don't need a mission statement or a purpose
I can be free to be me
because I've already been labeled obscene.

Trigger word Bit (TFF)

Tranny fucking faggot,
straight men are so offended
Is that your best insult?
Strain your brain through your asshole
Rappers Can't resist male homoerotic reference
Does this prove they are pussy eaters
and not cock enthusiasts.
Gain allure of fans, be famous and all that shit
I'm still a bit exhausted, smacking these lips
trying to will my delusions into flesh
Tranny fucking faggot weren't you a butch dyke
Why don't you go back to being
a straight chick for the dick?
Didn't you have some nice fat tits?

Tranny fucking faggot,
 did I steal those words before you thought them?
Or simply sourced the sass to ram
them back up your ass
Take it no KY
 the same way you dish out your wifi,
no password no hook up
Take it back to the park dogging from the trunk
Maybe you'll bend over for a load of my spunk

Tranny fucking faggot
 it's not an anthem but a dis track
To all those rappers who keep using that
You're not clever, unless you're advertising
Hoping to find true love to draw you
out of the closet

You Don't think this Tranny Fucking Faggot

can be famous?
It really doesn't matter what my name is
Someone some where has been screaming it
In bed at night it might be you dreaming it?

Rocky said don't dream it, be it.
      Tranny Fucking Faggot, how is it I still live?
Because I don't need your permission dip shit.

Strays

By rj Longren
9 tracks
Including
OUT GOLD,
spelling error,
Poor but rich in
heartache,
& a legend

Third album

These chemicals betray me,
 the tide rolls me over again
 the sleepless bellow of my sorrow tugging me
towards the bottom. I'm strapped in
A bit pale, growing thin, lungs folded over my skin
doing their best to reach oxygen
I'm inhaling,
I'm raising my capacity
waiting to see if it will do me in
Can't move a mountain in a sigh,
 whisper a defense against modern ambivalence

Will this year crack me?
Send me to the streets? Or simply cremate.
These things I still drag with me.
 Lucky unlucky duck my plastic roommate
I don't pull his string and he doesn't say a thing
Hold me humble to the time it takes to create poetry
Not every word is divinity
but unheard who would know anyway

My dip in hormones takes me down more roads
where I wet the pavement
Trying to spin out of control
taking my eyes from the paper
To never see the sun
might grant me hours in the glum
of my own resentment
Drink it in sour and piss it OUT GOLD,
that's what a true artist does isn't it?
Realized it's the zeal
at which the world might deface it.
Perhaps it's better to be dead
 than to become famous.

(Cancel Culture Grifter -previously released)
Can't cancel these rich men,
 they'll always reframe it
As me being offended and not as them fueling hatred
My trans femme sisters die in the streets
but rich men need to sell seats
Death brings dollar signs
while they memorialize the fresh meat
So sad suicide
but that couldn't have anything to do with me?
So says this rich man
I know I am powerful and I quit my tv show
Because I hated how it made me uncomfortable
reclaiming slurs
That white people thought they were all good
speaking those words
But hay I'm just going pick on a group
 weaker than me and jump on the outrage machine
Cha Ching.

i thought about seducing a random man to screw with him.
I thought about running my hands over his face,
making him blush and kiss me then slapping him.
choking him out and leaving him on the ground, the floor

What ever place i had gotten him 2 allow such nonsense.

Perhaps he is symbolic,
his small belly and one size up outfit

I haven't a home, a master or a steady love interest
I'm a mess, a stray at best,
tonight I might be your bae,
but in the morning I'll wake up a stray
I'm going to find a home
somewhere all these times I been hopeful and gay
I wore out these ruby slippers from my mouth,
 humorous no doubt
Skipping along the yellow bricks
trying to avoid sucking dicks
You'd be wiser they say if you weren't gay
Don't speak with a lisp, don't swish your hips
There's no love to be had unless god give you that path

I'm a mess, a stray lover, the random weekend guest
I been giving my affections away trying to stay
Head above water, drift don't waste the energy
trying to get loose from these bad dreams
Trying to speak my truth be genuine
Fame might make me the latest product line

Will I gather a new family from the stars in a richer galaxy
Or realize it's lonely anywhere that in my madness
I only imagine I need love to be happy

I'm moving the universe out of orbit testing gravity
Can I become the moon and the sun while collapsing?
Or I am the bleakness of time pulled out
From under the setting upending planets casually

I am the Author, My work is the new bible
Take my word as gospel, god whispers in my ear
He calls out when he comes, Drenching me in psalms
It's not going haunt you, the loss of me
I'm not willing to be sacrificed not the holy ghost
Not going bring it back like Jesus

on the **third track** he rose
Not the big GOD puppet master strings invisible to most
What would fame do but corrupt those it happens to
Gain wealth get your name out, hyped up bill board
Fashion line, concert tickets, cost a small automobile
Packed stands WE^ fucking ^ adore YOU
We worship that once you were poor too
It's fucked up and completely true
Can't pony up cash to buy followers, likes or sponsors
These lines I throw out feel like waste cans spit bait
Land me strange fragile empty day dreams
 if I do not implode than
I might survive another decade
I'll never be free in this roller coaster of haunted beams
The chunked up pavement I walked the wrong way down
Knowing it's not me, I can slide through this shit fine
Even if I keep landing ass out in a shallow stream
The hunks of mud keep me young
but recently I dared the heavens
Thinking god might hear me
 but he's too rich and I'm too gay

I am the Author,
there are only a few like me and every pen strokes my ego
As did Hemingway, Steinbeck, Joyce or Twain
it's all I know.

Will Grim Cracker find his Hannibal Lector?
Chase one another, tear limb for limb?
Lay spent in their graves, bones together
A dime a dozen these love stories

The sex is good because we're unglued
It seems he tore off a piece of me
Swallowed hard teeth stained
Can't wash out my taste with a parade

Cut up 4 confetti the organs I waste

It's a pretty line written here, out there it's a pity
All aired in public space

Will Grim Cracker find his Hannibal Lector?
Insert joke here about spreading cheeks and rectums
How dare I express a wish that contradicts
The heteronormative narrative I was not fully convinced
Would lead to happiness and life long bliss

You think I want to murder the American family?
The one on TV? Or the one that fucked up me?

Not so deep don't get hefty with this shit
Sometimes people can't handle it
They need the lube of a few naughty quips
A healthy handful of thick spit
A warm fingering of the opening
But what ever gateway the words bring

Will Grim Cracker be the nectar?
Or will he be fertilizer?

I disowned track five for being straight, it appears here.-
Grim Crack3r

I'm swimming in my loneliness imbibing it hard like mike
Slammed into a failed bet striving to stay upright

High **Five** before I take a nose dive
my luck might run dry
These urges got me thirsty, looking for some danger
In this universe
 I need to keep pushing my pen or nothing will exist
Misery is the thing that is most persistent

Slap it around again the phrase doesn't pay as it lays there
It tends to raise interest given who listens or spits it

In this life there's no one to rely on
Trust no man, trust no bitch
Not with love, not with secrets
How I wish this were fake
That people were compassionate
There is only me and when I forget
I'll be in this moment

I keep telling myself in this life
Trust no man, trust no bitch
Have your own back,

Have no regrets, save your heart from stitches

I might be an adrenaline junkie,
I'm swimming in unlucky driving into failure
Unashamed to have played with organs off grinder
Maybe five fingers get a discount, better lube up grandpa
words, like whores get used cheaply to set up my repeats
Are you worried about karma? That bitch never relents
Thank yourself for your own resilience

Let's talk dick, let's talk 6, let's talk numbers and letters
Switches in leathers,
up on the cross get off still strapped on
Self destruction is sweet, sweeter is the heat
Of a good forty licks on each ass cheek

That word bitch belongs in my mouth
Same as tranny, faggot I'll never forget
That my queerness has always been present
It fills you with dread but

I see you empty while I'm feeling alien
Loose in that sad sack of skin
Nail driven into the lid
Tight box sending lines
Across the web trap set
You look gullible boy snap
Those digits down, lettuce address
Not to impress but for failure
I admit I am lonely why does it matter
My lips give audience and body
am I too pretty?
To be playing in the gutter of humanity?
Grim cracking his knuckles letting vanity
Run rampant love the sincere draped nasty
Where would I hide if the foxes arrive?
Shed my skin and ascend into ether?
Slip my flesh and become vapor?
If I'm lethal than I'm the weapon
God uses to divide his people

Spelling error

C U empty I'm done in
This cold front on the whorizon is blowing my ass frozen
I'm a let it go ELSA style, low blow but
I'm getting too old for playing house
Even if you shove your mister out
Truth is I might have only wanted to make out.

Don't lean in to kiss me and miss me say
I CU empty, trying to get my fingers in your v a J J
But it's a spelling error thinking a finger or two will plug
the queer flood
That's coming down main street.

Shady mrs. Brady giggling CUNT
I see you drink up that Tea partied with drag queens
Spend your pin money on rainbow hooch and glitter
Getting, funny enough to LICK your besties' clit (er)
How dare abortion rights be tied to the trans plight
 making breeders' choices easy
RED their alt rights on a frequency
pitched under the guise of elite
Anything otherwise would be anarchy

"That's ENOUGH" I hear
"We are FED UP with all this We are Queer, we are here
Gay rights now U MF, Not next year.

It's a spelling error thinking the A stand for Ally
Thinking that you can deny us healthcare
while getting on your party
Taking it as your yearly good deed to support pride week

It's hard to be sweet while I'm hungry
and scared of dying on the street

CUNT I'm empty of caring about feeling so brave
Can't u see I'm always mad
because each week there's a new reason
Whether some state passes laws banning abortion
Or tells me which stall I can pee in,
 whether I pass or it does
There's no end in sight. Fuck you liberals cunts
Unwilling to denounce the religious right.

Poor but rich in heartache
Desperate but not selling out for corporate profit,
 capital gains
I know I might swerve in my lane,
hit the curb be blamed for debauchery
Talk shit because I'm ornery,
show my ass online thirsty, horny
This flesh still desires sex after all
Laying low off the alcohol
I'm a broke bitch this shit old
Rappers flashing stacks keeping their entourage warm
I'm nobody from nowhere midwest USA

You can keep the fame,
if the money rolls in I'll probably give it away
Being indifferent is a luxury,
neighborhoods swallowed up as trendy
No longer home to the gritty
 pain of the remnants left to search the city
No inch of pavement to call home
but somebody is making money

Poor but always fat with heartache
Desperate but not selling out to be the flavor of the week

What's my pitch to be registered in the struggle olympics?
What ditch did I dig myself up from?
Was I from a broken enough home?
To be fucked up inside, Creatively inclined,
depressed in my time
Emotional wreckage the fallout of left over resentments
Kept on a tight led with intentions of helping
The perceptions of white christians
Because there's limited roles available in the American
narrative

Poor but relaxed in my heartache
Snapped up the pen like blades of grass on the pond edge
Trying to not fall back into the water
Struggling when I was already near the bottom

America tries to seduce me
with lottery ticket dreams of fortune
Be famous and everything will have been worth it
Sell yourself like real estate, find the right buyer
Create a demand, violence can be the answer
Set yourself on fire
 and they will marvel at the momentary sparkle

If it were true I'd been a goner
Many times over when I was younger
Since I am this old I guess I will carry on
Being poor and heartbroken.

It was always about me, even if I call out to you
It's to bring you around to shield the world from my rage
To keep me from the stage where I destroy everything
If I can bring you close then I can taste hope
That it's not all ruined, my life
I want to blow up, hit the hard restart
Rather than collapse inward on my own heart
My plea to the powerful,
 that's the kind of pull to rip out the hull
Take this ship to the sea beyond the second star
and write my demands
Hold me fast to the ink of my pen as I list what remains
Am I a pawn in this game
Or the queen willing to sacrifice everything?
Am I to believe I am disposable ?
 Powerless and bear the brunt of mans disappointments
Am I a part of the dream?
A shadowy figure projected on a screen
You can't take from me what you never allowed me to have
The bare threads in my narrative frayed not for death
but for another season I wept
Took upon myself what ever helped.
Am I the prize to be sought or the closeted one?
This crown doesn't raise me to the heavens,
make me a divine presence
As god might anoint me with anything
 other than his spit for my persistence
Ink games and civil disobedience
as I lay awake in my residence

Alone in bed **a legend** playing out in my head
 I will rise with fierceness
Subject cracked the board using well placed words,
god heard
He said I don't give a fuck, what you do I'm a delusion too.
But it was nice you shared, please and thank you.

www.ingramcontent.com/pod-product-compliance
Lightning Source LLC
Chambersburg PA
CBHW061529250726
48657CB00005B/2157